DOT-TO-DOT DINOSAURS

Karen Bryant-Mole

Illustrated By Graham Round

Edited by Jenny Tyler

First life

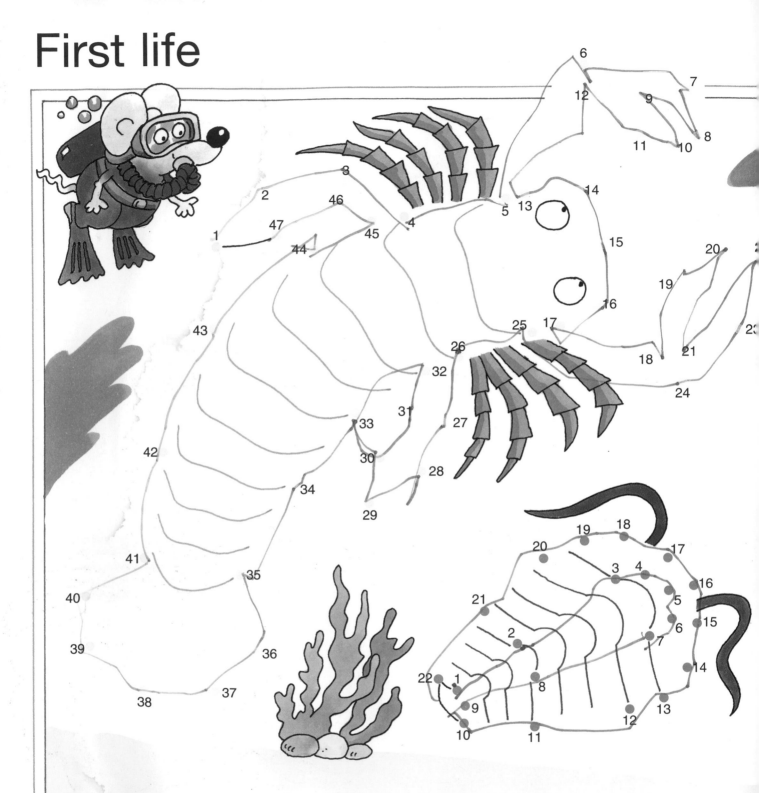

Life on our planet began in the sea.

- Join the blue dots to see one of the first animals. It is called a trilobite.

- Join the orange dots to see an animal which you can still find in the sea today.

1 2 3 4 5 6 7 8 9 10 11 12 13 14 15 16 17 18 19 20 21 22 23 24 25

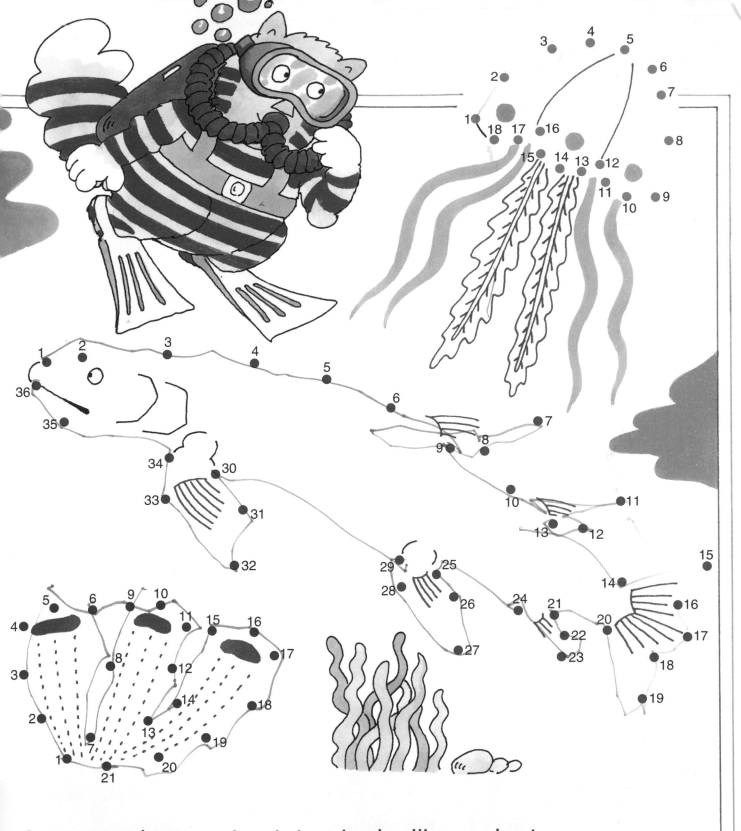

A sponge is an animal that looks like a plant.
Join the purple dots to find one.

Join the red dots to see a prehistoric fish.

You can see a sea scorpion by joining the yellow dots.

Life comes ashore

Some of the first land animals were fish which developed lung and strong fins to pull themselves along the ground.

- Join the green dots to see a lung fish called Eusthenopteron

- Join the blue dots to see Ichthyostega, which was an amphibian. Amphibians can live both on land and in water

51 52 53 54 55 56 57 58 59 60 61 62 63 64 65 66 67 68 69 70 71 72 73 74 75

There were lots of giant insects around at this time too.

- Join the red dots to see a cockroach, the yellow dots to see a spider and the purple dots to see a huge dragonfly.
- Can you find cat and mouse?

The first reptiles

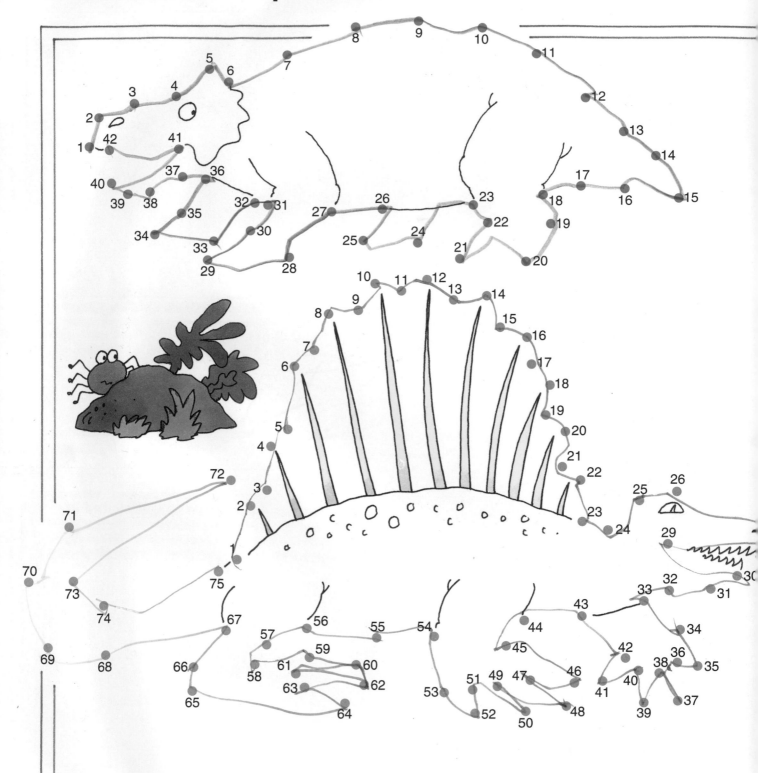

The next group of animals to appear were the reptiles.
Reptiles have dry, scaly skins and lay eggs with shells.

- Join the green dots to find Pareiasaurus. This was one
  of the first plant-eating reptiles.

1 2 3 4 5 6 7 8 9 10 11 12 13 14 15 16 17 18 19 20 21 22 23 24 25

- Join the yellow dots to see an Araeoscelis.

Some of the reptiles had large sails on their backs. These probably helped them to warm up by soaking up the sun's rays.

- Join the blue dots to see Dimetrodon, which ate meat.
  Join the red dots to see Edaphosaurus, which ate plants.

Early dinosaurs

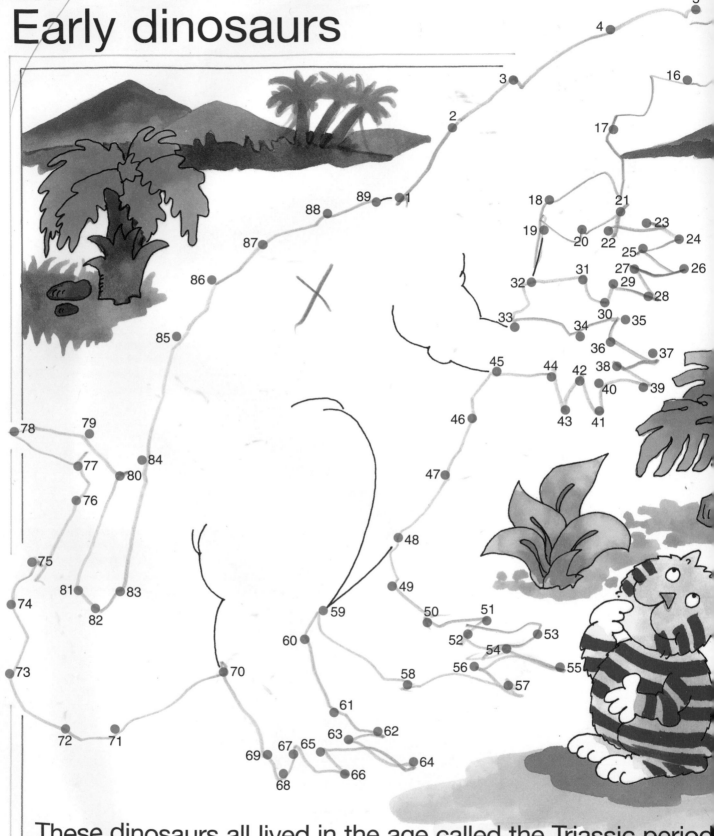

These dinosaurs all lived in the age called the Triassic period

- Join the blue dots to see a tiny dinosaur called Saltopus
- If you join the green dots you will see a big Plateosaurus.

51 52 53 54 55 56 57 58 59 60 61 62 63 64 65 66 67 68 69 70 71 72 73 74 7

- Coelophysis was slim with a long neck and tail. Join the yellow dots to see what it looked like.

- The dinosaur you see when you join the red dots is called Anchisaurus.

The giants

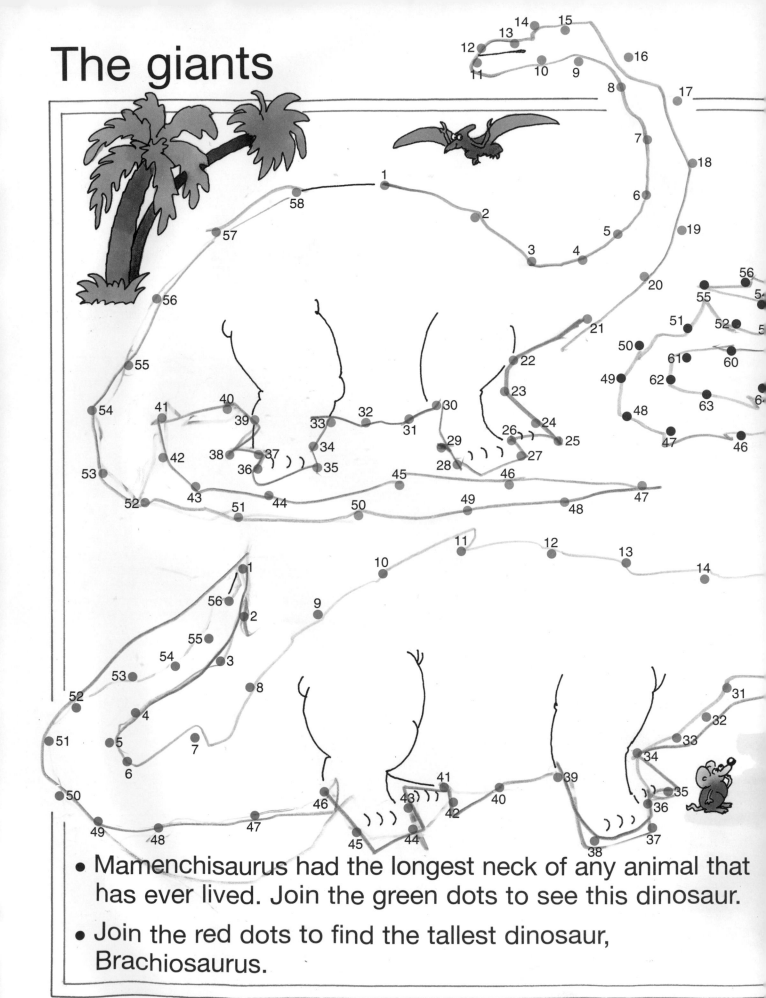

- Mamenchisaurus had the longest neck of any animal that has ever lived. Join the green dots to see this dinosaur.
- Join the red dots to find the tallest dinosaur, Brachiosaurus.

1 2 3 4 5 6 7 8 9 10 11 12 13 14 15 16 17 18 19 20 21 22 23 24 25

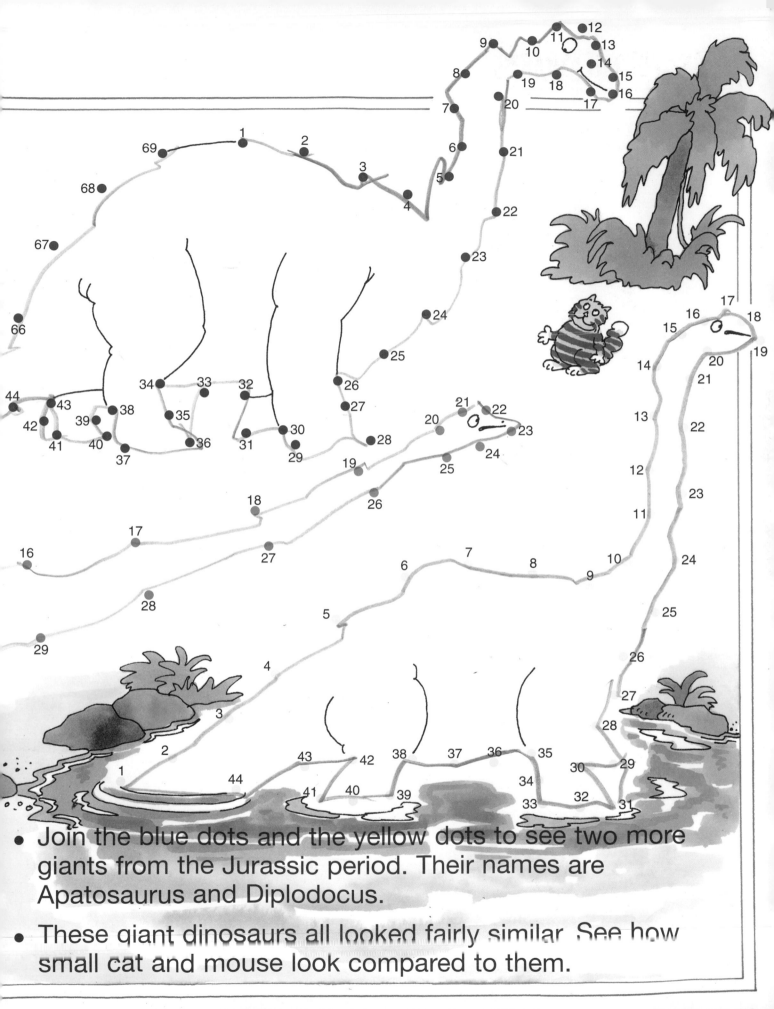

- Join the blue dots and the yellow dots to see two more giants from the Jurassic period. Their names are Apatosaurus and Diplodocus.

- These giant dinosaurs all looked fairly similar. See how small cat and mouse look compared to them.

26 27 28 29 30 31 32 33 34 35 36 37 38 39 40 41 42 43 44 45 46 47 48 49 50

By the water

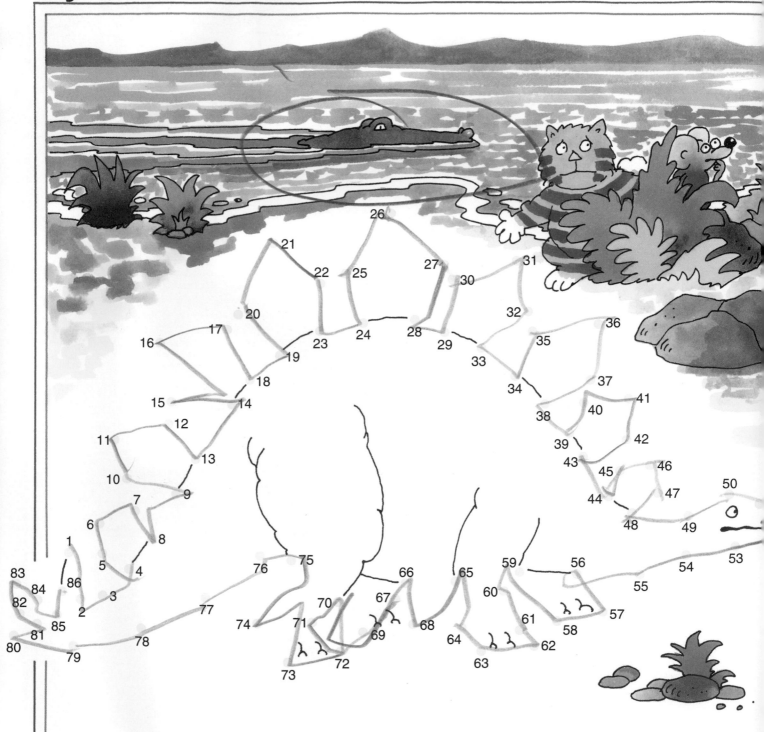

- Cat has spotted Allosaurus, one of the main meat-eating Jurassic dinosaurs. Join the red dots to see it.

- Join the green dots to see Compsognathus which was only the size of a hen.

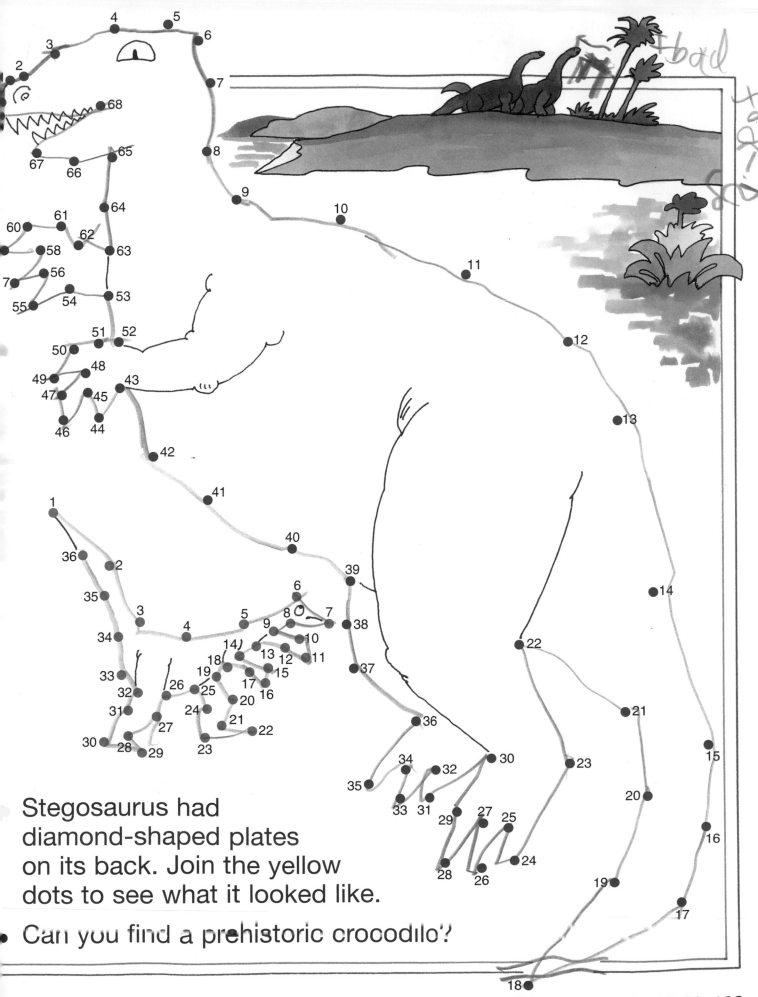

Stegosaurus had
diamond-shaped plates
on its back. Join the yellow
dots to see what it looked like.

Can you find a prehistoric crocodile?

In the air

Flying reptiles are called pterosaurs.

- Join the green dots to see the pterosaur Dimorphodon.
- Join the orange dots to find another pterosaur called Rhamphorhynchus.

1 2 3 4 5 6 7 8 9 10 11 12 13 14 15 16 17 18 19 20 21 22 23 24 25

Pterodactylus was a small pterosaur. It was about the size of a starling. Join the red dots to see one.

If you join the blue dots you will see Archaeopteryx. Many people say that it was the first real bird.

26 27 28 29 30 31 32 33 34 35 36 37 38 39 40 41 42 43 44 45 46 47 48 49 50

Sea monsters

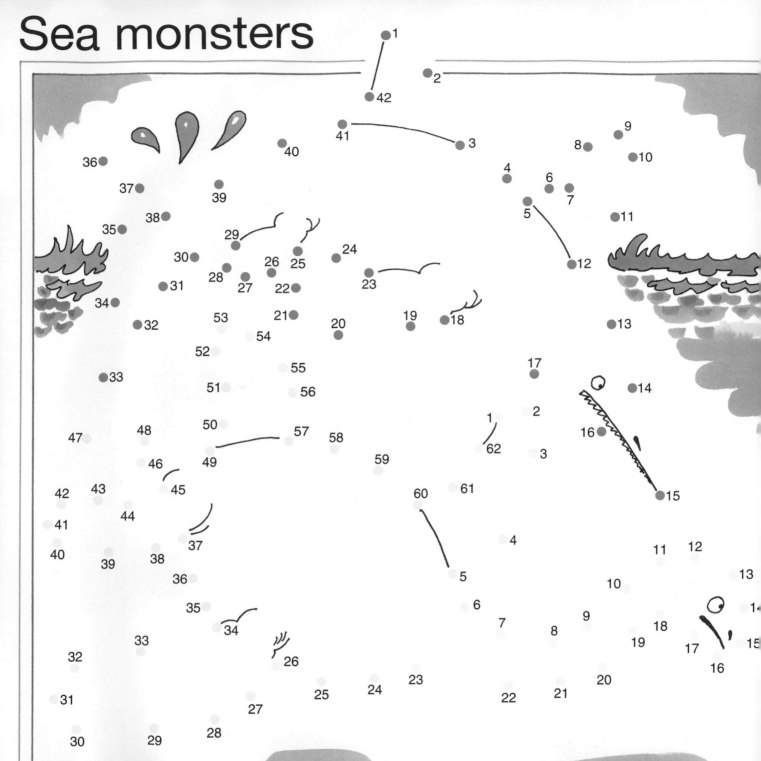

Plesiosaurs and pliosaurs were sea reptiles which lived at the same time as dinosaurs.

- Join the yellow dots to find a long-necked plesiosaur called Cryptoclidus.
- Join the blue dots to see a pliosaur called Liopleurodon.

If you join the green dots you will find an Ichthyosaurus. Its name means "fish lizard".

Join the red dots to see the enormous turtle, Archelon.

Plated dinosaurs

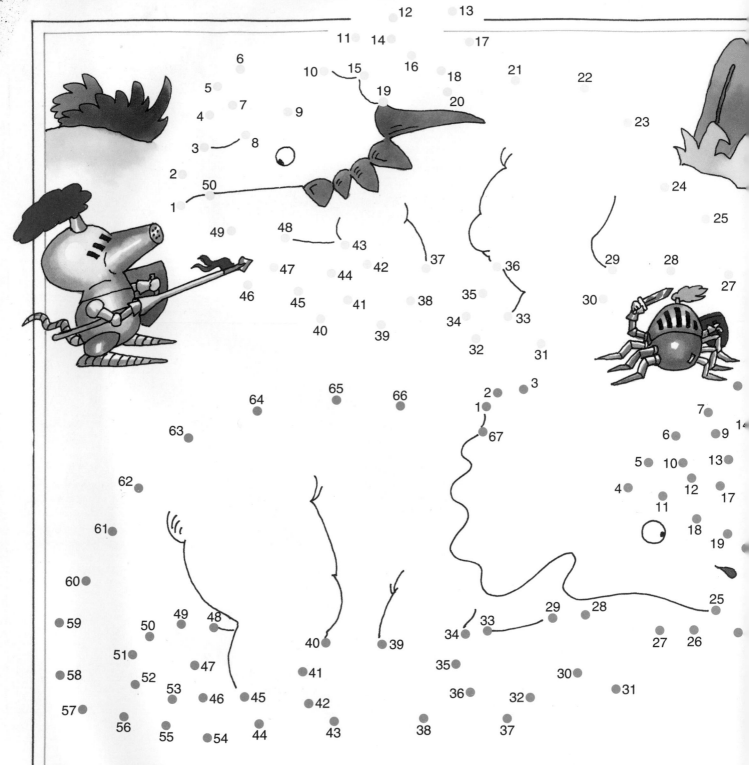

Some of the dinosaurs had protective plates to shield them from other dinosaurs.

- Join the blue dots to see Triceratops and the yellow dots to find Styracosaurus.

1 2 3 4 5 6 7 8 9 10 11 12 13 14 15 16 17 18 19 20 21 22 23 24 25

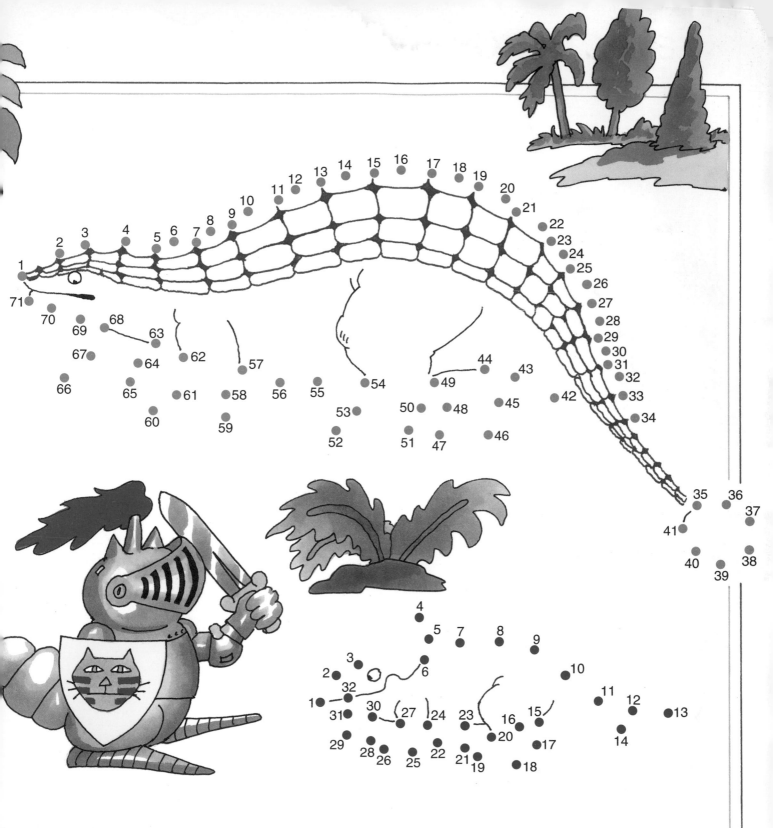

Ankylosaurus was covered in bony plates.
It used the large bones on the end of its tail as a club.
Join the green dots to see one.

Join the red dots to see a small dinosaur called Protoceratops.

More large dinosaurs

- Tyrannosaurus was probably the fiercest of all the dinosaurs. Find out what it looked like by joining the yellow dots.

- Parasaurolophus had a long bony crest on its head. Join the green dots to see this strange dinosaur.

51 52 53 54 55 56 57 58 59 60 61 62 63 64 65 66 67 68 69 70 71 72 73 74 7

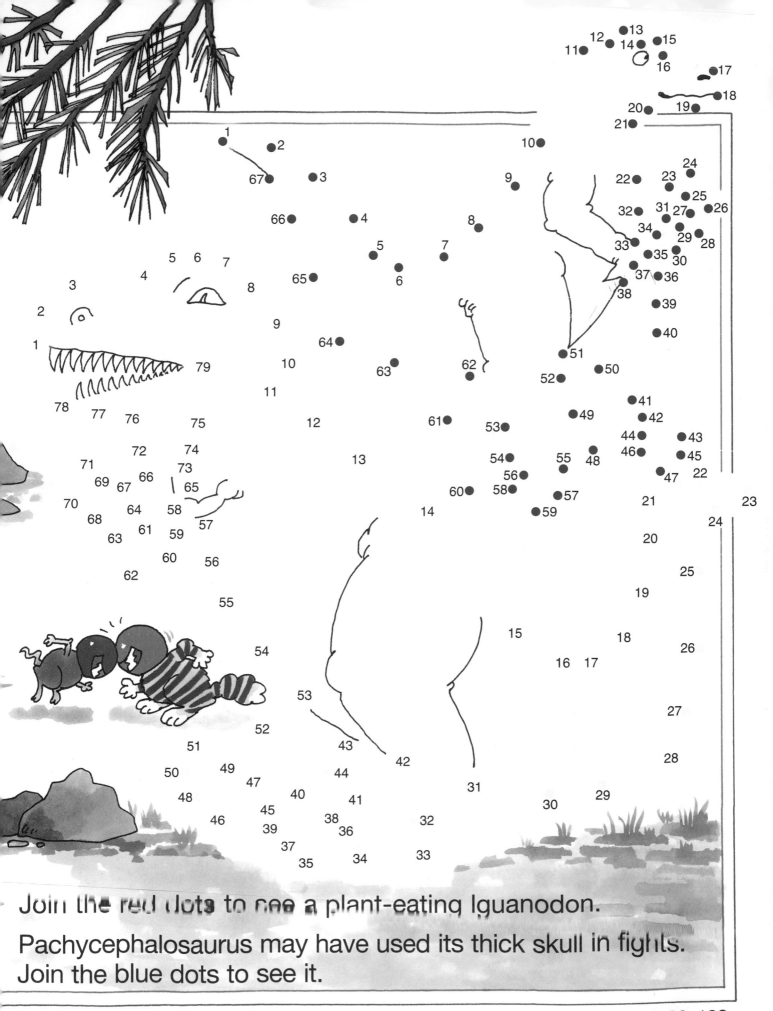

Join the red dots to see a plant-eating Iguanodon.

Pachycephalosaurus may have used its thick skull in fights.
Join the blue dots to see it.

Some smaller dinosaurs

Here are some dinosaurs that look fairly similar.

- Join the red dots to see the long-tailed Ornithomimus.

- Stenonychosaurus was one of the most intelligent dinosaurs. You can find one by joining the yellow dots.

1 2 3 4 5 6 7 8 9 10 11 12 13 14 15 16 17 18 19 20 21 22 23 24 25

Join the blue and green dots.
One of these dinosaurs is called Deinonychus and eats meat with its sharp teeth. The other is a plant-eater with a bony beak called Hypsllophodon. Which is which?

Saying the names

Allosaurus
Al-oh-saw-rus

Coelophysis
See-low-fy-sis

Eusthenopteron
Yews-then-op-tur-on

Ornithomimus
Or-nith-oh-my-mus

Saltopus
Salt-oh-puss

Anchisaurus
An-kee-saw-rus

Compsognathus
Komp-sog-nay-thus

Hypsilophodon
Hips-ill-offa-don

Pachycephalosaurus
Pak-ee-sef-al-oh-saw-rus

Stegosaurus
Steg-oh-saw-rus

Ankylosaurus
An-ky-low-saw-rus

Cryptoclidus
Krip-oh-kly-dus

Ichthyostega
Ik-thee-oh-saw-rus

Parasaurolophus
Para-saw-rollo-fuss

Stenonychosaurus
Sten-on-ik-oh-saw-rus

Apatosaurus
A-pat-oh-saw-rus

Deinonychus
Dy-non-ee-kus

Ichthyostega
Ik-thee-oh-stee-ga

Pareiasaurus
Par-eye-a-saw-rus

Styracosaurus
Sty-rack-oh-saw-rus

Araeoscelis
A-ray-oh-sell-iss

Dimetrodon
Dee-mee-tro-don

Iguanodon
Ig-wa-no-don

Plateosaurus
Plat-ee-oh-saw-rus

Triceratops
Try-ser-a-tops

Archaepteryx
Are-kee-op-tur-iks

Dimorphodon
Die-more-foe-don

Iguanodon
Ig-wa-no-don

Protoceratops
Pro-toe-ser-a-tops

Trilobite
Try-low-bite

Archelon
Ar-ke-lon

Diplodocus
Dip-lo-doe-kus

Liopleurodon
Lee-oh-plu-roe-don

Pterodactylus
Ter-oh-dak-til-us

Brachiosaurus
Brack-ee-oh-saw-rus

Edaphosaurus
Eda-foe-saw-rus

Mamenchisaurus
Ma-men-ke-saw-rus

Rhamphorhynchus
Ram-foe-rin-kus

Tyrannosaurus
Tie-ran-oh-saw-rus